© Brain Mike 2020

All rights reserved. No part of this publication may be reproduced, stored in a retrieval system, or transmitted in any form or by any means, electronic, mechanical, photocopying, recording, or otherwise, without the prior written permission of the author.

Contents

Chapter 1 1

Introduction to Metal Detecting 1

   Metal Detecting Basic Theory You Need to know 2

   Short Working Principle of Metal Detector 3

   My Journey to Metal Detecting Hobby 3

   Types of Metal Detector 5

   Beat-frequency Oscillator metal detector 5

   What is the Beauty of Beat-frequency Oscillator Metal Detectors? ... 6

   Very Low Frequency metal detector 7

   Pulse Induction Metal Detector (PI) 8

   Why Do People have Interest in Metal Detecting? 9

   Tips for Metal Detecting 10

Chapter 2 12

Understanding the Metal Detecting Lingo and Guide 12

   Using Your Metal Detector Right During Treasure Hunt 18

Chapter 3 22

Rules and Getting Permission for Metal Detecting 22

   Can a detectorist be punished for not observing metal detecting rules? 23

   The Rules of Metal Detecting Explained 23

   How can I get Permission to Detect on A Land? 25

Chapter 4 28

Mastering Your Metal Detector 28

   Assembling and Understanding Your Metal Detector 32

   Is it Right to Change My Metal Detector Frequently? 32

Troubleshooting in Metal Detector 33

The Impacts of Minerals on Metal Detectors 34

Chapter 5 35

Classifications of Metal Detectors 35

Minelab Metal Detectors 35

Bounty Hunter Metal Detectors 37

Bounty Hunter Pioneer EX Metal Detector 39

Teknetics Metal Detectors 41

Can Teknetics metal detectors find Gold? 41

Is Teknetics metal detectors good for beginners? 41

Fisher Lab Metal Detectors 42

Garrett Metal Detectors 43

Garrett ACE 250 Metal Detectors 43

Hunting with Garrett ACE 250 Metal Detector as a Beginner 44

Chapter 6 45

Safety and Relics Metal Detecting 45

Safety Precautions in Metal Detecting 46

Relic Metal Detectors 48

Garrett ACE 400 for Relics Metal Detecting 49

Chapter 7 50

Coin Shooting and Metal Detectors for Other Areas 50

Metal Detectors for Coins Shooting 51

Tips in Coin Shooting and Coins Maintenance 51

Where can I go to coin shooting? 52

Underwater Metal Detecting 53

Underwater Metal Detectors 53

Minelab Excalibur II Underwater Metal Detector 54

Gold Detecting 55

Where can Gold be detected? 56

Metal Detectors for Gold Detecting 56

Multipurpose Metal Detectors 58

Chapter 8 60

Detecting in Water, Treasure Identification and Other Teachings 60

What are the possible Treasures to be discovered in Rivers and Oceans? 61

Metal Detecting in Beach 61

Beach Metal Detectors 63

Identifying Your Finds with Metal Detector Feature 63

Guide on Identifying Your Coins 65

How to identify Relics 66

How to identify Jewelries 66

Accessories Needed for Metal Detecting 67

How to recover a Target 70

Making Good Research before Treasure Hunt Outing 71

Chapter 9 73

Enhancing Your Detecting Skill, Cleaning and Selling Your Finds 73

Joining Metal Detecting Club 74

How to clean Your Found Coins 75

Step by Step Guide on Cleaning your Detected Jewelry 77

How to Clean Up Your Gold Find 77

Cleaning Iron Relics Using Electrolysis Method 77

How to preserve Your Iron Relics 79

How to sell Your Finds 79

Appreciation 81

Index 82

Chapter 1

Introduction to Metal Detecting

Metal detecting can be defined as the processing of finding valuable metals with the use of a principal tool called metal detector. Metal detecting is a nice hobby though it can be demanding sometimes. Some valuable finds that are discovered during metal detecting are made of Gold, Quartz, Magnetite, Diamond and Silver. Metal detectors were primarily designed to detect Gold but today can detect many other valuable metals.

In this book, I will cover the knowledge you need to gain ground in metal detecting, the best locations, different kinds of metal detectors for detecting different kinds of finds, ground evaluation before detecting and many more. I will also guide you on the equipment you need to embark on metal detecting successfully. There are many things you need to know. I will take them part by part.

Metal Detecting Basic Theory You Need to know

The word "theory" implies a set of principles on which the practice of an activity is based. You need to know about this theory to help you in your treasure hunt. If you do not have the basic foundational ideas in a particular area of interest, you may end up not getting it right at the end.

Without metal detector, there is no metal detecting. So, metal detector is the key tool. A metal detector is an electronic machine used to detect metals buried long time ago under the ground which can be gold, silver, artifacts/relics and old coins of value. When a metal detector detects the presence of these treasurable metals, it gives notification which can come as vibrations or audible beeps.

The metals of value can be found in beaches, oceans, rivers, woods. forests, parks, rocks, abandoned homes and locations where wars occurred years back. These locations from my experience over the years are good locations to find metal treasures.

A metal detector is made of a metal handle and a sensor. These two parts are the two major parts of the machine. The sensor does the real work. When you sweep through the ground while hunting for metals, once the sensor comes across any metal which it is sensitive to, it beeps. This is to notify you that there is a metal hidden underground. For more advanced metal detectors, different metal gives different beep sound.

The distance between a metal target and the sensor has a way it affects the beeps. The closer the metal target is, the louder the beeps. And the farer the distance between the metal target to the sensor, the lower the beeps sound from the detector. As a result of this factor, you are to pay good attention to beeps as you search for metals so that you do not lose good finds. Also wearing headphone will be of good help.

Short Working Principle of Metal Detector

It will not sound good to have a metal detector without knowing the science behind its operation. So, let us look into it. A metal detector works through electromagnetic effect. The electromagnetic field in the metal detector coils is transmitted into the ground when searching for metal. Whenever the field encounters a metal target, the electromagnetic field from the coils energizes the target and it becomes charged and hence transmit their own electromagnetic field. In this state, the detector search coil receives the retransmitted electromagnetic field and you as the user of the metal detector hears the beep which implies that a metal is detected.

My Journey to Metal Detecting Hobby

My father was a metal detecting hobbyist. He usually made some finds those years he was actively involved in the hobby. As a little child, I didn't like seeing my father leave the house when he was done with his duty at his workplace. But, for the fact that he likes metal detecting, I had no choice than to let him do what he cherished. When he was on leave, he did go for hunt of treasures in the morning and in the evening. He was a successful metal detecting hobbyist because he made some good finds.

As I was growing, I sometimes used his metal detector to search around the environment where we were leaving because he at a point taught me how to use the machine. Because I was still new in the practice then (about 16 years old then) I did not make any valuable find. But I did not give up.

The real thing happened when I was 18 years of age. My father took me into a forest for metal detecting. As of then, he bought a metal detector for me. I cannot remember the manufacturer of that metal detector, but it was a sound one because it was sensitive to metal materials.

On that faithful day when we got to the forest, he directed me to the location I was to face while he was still within the same environment (not too far from me). As I was making my search, I came to a spot and my metal detector beeped. It sounded in my ear as if it was not real, but I swept my search coil on that spot again and still heard the audio sound. I was happy but on the other hand I asked myself "what if what is under this ground is just a metal scrap"?

I summoned courage and began to dig the ground. I applied the necessary caution which my father taught me in order not to damage the target. Do you know what I found under the ground? I found relic which has cultural and historical value. My daddy was happy with me.

After our outing, when we got home, he cleaned the finds we got for the day. He did not know how valuable the relic which I detected was until he went out to sell it including the other finds. He got cool cash from the find and bought something nice for me from part of the money. As from that day, my passion for finding treasures increased. I can boldly tell you that I am a successful metal detecting hobbyist.

Types of Metal Detector

Any type of metal detector you have seen or planning to buy falls into any of the three main categories of metal detector. In this section, I will walk you through to understand these three systems and where they work best.

The three main types of metal detector systems are:

1. Beat-frequency Oscillator metal detector
2. Very Low Frequency metal detector and
3. Pulse Induction Metal detector

Beat-frequency Oscillator metal detector

The Beat-frequency Oscillator metal detector is usually represented with the acronym "BFO". The system used in building this type of metal detectors happens to be the oldest and basic in history. Metal detectors that work with BFO are simple and basic and as a result of that it is recommended for beginners. So, you can start with this type of metal detector as a beginner.

Metal detectors build with this technology has six modified analog circuit which comprises one digital circuit and many basic components. The BFO metal detector comes with headphone jack. In old BFO metal detectors, the headphone jack is of 1/4" but in the modern time, is about 3.5mm.

Explaining how Beat-frequency Oscillator metal detector works, it operates with two radio frequency oscillators. The two radio frequencies are to be slightly different from each other to produce the expected result.

One of the radio oscillators is known as the search oscillator and the other is reference oscillator. It is the collaboration of these two oscillators that give audible beeps during metal detecting.

When you are in the field trying to detect metals and a metal interferes with the magnetic field of the search coil, the frequency of the search oscillator adjusts slightly, and the detector will produce a signal in the audio frequency range.

What is the Beauty of Beat-frequency Oscillator Metal Detectors?

What I mean in this subheading is the good thing about BFO metal detectors. The good thing about metal detectors produced with this technology are as follow:

1. Beat-frequency Oscillator metal detectors are inexpensive

2. Metal detectors manufactured with BFO technology are simple to handle

Very Low Frequency metal detector

This is another type of metal detector based on the technology used to produce it. Very low frequency metal detectors are the most popular metal detectors found in the market today. With this detector, you can find metallic treasures. This metal detector gives more accurate result than BFO metal detectors which has this as disadvantage. Very low frequency metal detectors are also known with the abbreviation **VLF** metal detectors.

VLF metal detectors are also known as induction balance. The detector is built with two major set of coils. These coils are **transmitter** and **receiver** coils. Transmitter coil is the outer coil loop of the detector. The coil is made of electric wires. In the electric wire coil, electricity is sent into it in one direction first and later in another direction. Electricity passes through the wire coil thousands of times in each second.

On the other hand, the receiver coil is the inner coil of the detector which is built with coil of wire. The wire coil acts as an antenna to pick up and then amplify frequencies that comes from the metallic treasure buried in the ground.

At low frequency, metal detectors of this type become sensitive to valuable metal targets. This is because low frequencies penetrate the ground deeper than high.

Metal detectors built with Very Low Frequency technology has discrimination property when searching for treasures. That is to say that this kind of metal detectors can discriminate between desirable metals from those which are not needed. Very low frequency metal detectors can be used to easily detect gold, silver and copper in the ground. In terms of detecting length, VLF metal detectors can find treasures that are 15cm deep in the ground.

Pulse Induction Metal Detector (PI)

This type of metal detector works with pulse effect. In metal detectors of this type, powerful, short bursts (pulses) of current are sent through a coil of wire. Each of the pulses generates a brief magnetic field. PI metal detector has single coil which functions both the receiver and transmitter. They are good metal detectors for hunting for treasures in mineralized grounds. So, if you plan to hunt in such locations, go for this kind of metal detector. This type of metal detector is built with sound discrimination property. The metal detector is good to hunt in salt-water exploration because the material in such location is highly conductive in the soil.

Why Do People have Interest in Metal Detecting?

There are different reasons why people go into metal detecting. Some people are hunting precious metals today because of their love for the hobby. Some others still embark on it because of the financial benefit. Your own reason may be different.

One day, I got into discussion with Richard, a fellow metal hobbyist on the subject matter. I asked him why he is into metal detecting. Richard answered that he likes it because whenever he discovers small golds, that his heart is always filled with joy. He went on and said that the exercise is tiring but remembering what stands ahead always makes him feel cool.

Richards target is always gold. As a result of that, he always goes for metal detectors produced to target gold as the main metal of interest. That is to tell you that there are different metal detectors for different metal finds. If your target is diamond or silver, you can ask the detector seller of that before buying but I will explain some to you as I go on.

People go into metal detecting because they want to make few dollars from their finds. This is one of the major reasons' detectorists from United States and United Kingdom go into metal detecting. The money made from metal treasures can be motivating sometimes depending on how the metals are valued. Old coins of value can put smiles on your face.

When I met an old couple in the site where I was hunting for hidden treasures, I wondered why they were still finding treasures at that age.

I engaged them into short discussion on why still going out for metal detecting. The husband to the woman, Mr. Peter, spoke up. He said that such outing makes them feel good because it was a way of exercising their body systems. He went further and made it clear that anytime they go out and hunt, they usually feel better in the night because of the exercise involved.

There are many reasons people go for metal detecting but let me tell you, metal detecting is rewarding when you make good finds. As you begin your search, just hope for something good. Your name may appear in your national newspaper because of the find you make. So, in all, metal detecting is good.

Tips for Metal Detecting

Let me share some ideas you need to make good finds. As a beginner, getting reasonable finds at a start can be difficult but luck may smile at you. I have to quickly share some tips which I believe will keep you going and make your treasure hunt less stressful.

To have fruitful metal detecting outing, take these tips:

1. Go for metal detecting with the right tools
2. Practice good listening culture
3. Know your target and because of that go with the best metal detector
4. Understand the location you are planning to hunt
5. Study location map

6. Study the history of your target location
7. Do not trespass
8. Observe safety measures
9. Search for long duration
10. Take your detector close enough to the ground surface
11. Hunt after rain when the ground is wet

Chapter 2

Understanding the Metal Detecting Lingo and Guide

Every profession has the jargon they use to communicate with one another. That of metal detecting is not going to be different. For the fact that metal detecting hobbyists are involved, these jargons must continue to be used by the hunters of treasures.

The word 'lingo' simply implies terms that metal detecting hobbyists use among one another. Sometimes they know it within themselves. When they communicate in some cases, an outsider hardly understands them. As a beginner, you are to know about these terms. You may find yourself among experienced metal hunters tomorrow. And you know it will not be nice for you to get lost in their midst.

Because of the importance, I will guide you through in knowing some of them. But, without you knowing, I have mentioned few of these terms in chapter 1. The few includes BFO, which stands for Beat-frequency Oscillator metal detector, VLF which means Very Low

Frequency metal detector, and PI which stands for Pulse Induction metal detector.

Let me go on and explain terms in metal detecting for you:

All metal

This term applies to metal detecting machine. When you turn your metal detector to all metal mode, it implies that the discrimination property of the detector will not work. A metal detector in all metal mode detects every metal object it comes across in the course of the hunt including junk.

Tone ID

The tone ID is also a lingo that is used for metal detector. It is an audio tone which any metal detected is known with. For example, Gold may have high tone ID and Iron artifact has low tone ID. Tone ID can vary depending on the target material. But with time and careful study, you will master the tone ID for gold, silver, diamond and other metallic materials.

Visual ID

A visual ID is a property of metal detector that allows you to picture the metal detected in the ground before you go on with digging. This feature is integrated into modern day manufactured metal detectors as a result of advancement in technology. It is a welcomed development to us treasure hunters because it has helped us got more valuable metals instead of wasting our energy digging trash.

Choppy

This is an audio metal detector gives when it detects a metal that is almost discriminated out through the settings mode of the machine. This signal sounds questionable, but it is advised you still dig to find out the real content.

Find

It is treasure you discovered during metal detecting that is worth keeping. It can be gold necklace, ring or any other metallic treasure you want to keep. I use this term frequently during treasure hunt.

Low tone

This is the low sound metal detectors produce when they detect metal treasure that have low conductivity property. Example of such metals are gold and pull tabs.

Bling

This is the term we use to define fancy jewelry. This metal may or may not be precious metals. When you detect this metal at first you are likely to be confused of its state because of its appearance. The best bling is a jewelry which is loaded with valuable metal.

Black dirt

This is a sand type usually found in old sites. When you dig a hole during metal detecting and you are close to this kind of sand, you are likely to discover at least a sound treasure. When I am on a site trying to find treasure, once I find this sand during the exercise, I am usually happy. Black dirt is rich soil.

Black sand

Black sand is another type of sand that is marked for something nice. When you find black sand during this precious hobby, it is an indication that you are close to gold. This kind of sand is rich in iron particles.

Bucketlister

Do you sense the way the word sounds? If you examine the word properly, you will find out that it was formed from the combination of two main words; "bucket and lister". A bucketlister is a remarkable find you discovered during metal detecting that is very spectacular. Maybe you never for once thought of coming across such find in your life but happened in a day.

Cache

A cache simply implies a group of coins or jewelry buried by a group of persons in a particular place long time ago. During metal detecting, any hobbyist that comes across them makes real money from them. They are sometimes buried in jars. Also, they are close to each other to where they are buried. So, if someone tells you that he discovered cache, I believe you know what the term is?

Cache hunting

The above term was derived from two major words; "cache and hunting ". From that combination, cache hunting is treasure hunt for cluster of coins or other previous treasures that are clustered. In this kind of hunting, special approach and study is applied to get the expected result.

Coinball

Coinball can mean different thing to different people depending on the discipline the term is used. In metal detecting, coinball mean something unique. A coin ball is dirt with coins hidden inside. So, if you are pinpointing and your machine beeps, just hold on and find out what is inside the dirt. There may be expensive coins inside.

Canslaw

This is defined as a set of Aluminum cans scattered around a particular area because they were hit by lawnmower. These cans make metal detecting in that area difficult because the Aluminum which are of different sizes give variety of signals.

Color

In metal detecting hobby, we use color to describe gold. If you are hunting on a particular area and you tell someone that you unearthed color as a treasure, automatically you have discovered Gold.

Clad

to find treasure, once I find this sand during the exercise, I am usually happy. Black dirt is rich soil.

Black sand

Black sand is another type of sand that is marked for something nice. When you find black sand during this precious hobby, it is an indication that you are close to gold. This kind of sand is rich in iron particles.

Bucketlister

Do you sense the way the word sounds? If you examine the word properly, you will find out that it was formed from the combination of two main words; "bucket and lister". A bucketlister is a remarkable find you discovered during metal detecting that is very spectacular. Maybe you never for once thought of coming across such find in your life but happened in a day.

Cache

A cache simply implies a group of coins or jewelry buried by a group of persons in a particular place long time ago. During metal detecting, any hobbyist that comes across them makes real money from them. They are sometimes buried in jars. Also, they are close to each other to where they are buried. So, if someone tells you that he discovered cache, I believe you know what the term is?

Cache hunting

The above term was derived from two major words; "cache and hunting ". From that combination, cache hunting is treasure hunt for cluster of coins or other previous treasures that are clustered. In this kind of hunting, special approach and study is applied to get the expected result.

Coinball

Coinball can mean different thing to different people depending on the discipline the term is used. In metal detecting, coinball mean something unique. A coin ball is dirt with coins hidden inside. So, if you are pinpointing and your machine beeps, just hold on and find out what is inside the dirt. There may be expensive coins inside.

Canslaw

This is defined as a set of Aluminum cans scattered around a particular area because they were hit by lawnmower. These cans make metal detecting in that area difficult because the Aluminum which are of different sizes give variety of signals.

Color

In metal detecting hobby, we use color to describe gold. If you are hunting on a particular area and you tell someone that you unearthed color as a treasure, automatically you have discovered Gold.

Clad

This is a desirable coin in the absence of old valuable coins. They are new coins formulated with non-precious metals. These coins are designed in Silver color in the United States.

Coin Spill

This is bad experience detectorists usually encounter though it does not happen always. Coin spill is when a coin spills out of the bag of a hobbyist after or during detecting. This usually happens due to the carelessness of the treasure hunter. To avoid having this ugly experience, always go with good and deep bag. It is better to be careful than to lose the value you discovered after a long day.

Pennyweight

Pennyweight is a unit of measurement that is equal to 24 grams. It is abbreviated dwt, d standing for denarius an ancient Roman coin

Pinpointer

A pinpointer is hand-held metal detector which is small in size. It is used inside of an opened hole/plug to help locate targets. When you dig a ground and you get to a point where you want to get to the specific direction of the treasure you are looking for, you are to use pinpointer. The act of using pinpointer to detect treasure is called pinpointing.

Assay

Being also a term used in the field of metal detecting, assay is a metallurgy process that can be used to identify the purity of a treasure.

Detectorists use it to find out whether any found treasure like Gold, Silver or any other is pure or not. Proportions of precious metal are discovered through essay.

Plug

Plug is a hole that is properly and carefully dug during metal detecting. A good plug is usually the work of an experienced metal detectorist. A treasure hunter who digs a plug saves the ground from destruction and such practice is encouraged.

Tot-lot

The name might sound funny to you, but our interest is in knowing what it is. Tot lot is a playground for very young children. The place is designed in a way to prevent children from injury and is usually located close to parks. It is also a place for lost jewelries. As a result of this, many metal detecting hobbyists visit such locations.

Relic Hunters

As the name implies, these are metal enthusiasts who specialize in detecting relics. For this kind of treasure hunters, their searches occur in fields or woods and usually target areas that reflect early conflicts such as places that experienced Civil War in the United States.

Using Your Metal Detector Right During Treasure Hunt

There are some things you are to take care of during metal detecting. Also, there are some things you have to take into consideration when you go out to hunt for treasures. Do not think that because you have metal detector that you can use it to do anything you want to do. DO NOT ABAUSE THE USE OF METAL DETECTORS….

Things you need to know:

Carrying and searching

The way you carry and move with your metal detector is important during your hunt for treasures. When hunting for treasures make sure you keep your search coil height approximately 1 to 2 inches and your detector must be parallel to the ground for effective results. Do not raise your search coil too much so that it will easily establish connection with the target under the ground.

Your Movement

Do not be in a haste when you are in the field to hunt for treasures. Try and take it easy and move gradually. If you rush, you may rush out from the treasure you would have found. As you take your steps, move your search coil at a speed of about 2 to 5 feet per second.

Cover Holes

Many metal detecting hobbyists are guilty of this. As a beginner, you do not need to follow bad example. Just go for the good. If you go out to hunt for treasures with your metal detector and during this exercise dig some holes, please cover them up. That will make the lands organized and look neat.

Do not Destroy Properties

That you are given the opportunity to hunt on a person's land does not give you license to destroy other valuable things inside there. Do not destroy plants and animal lives. Also, do not destroy any other things of value. Even if you do due to mistake, let the owner know.

Trash management

When digging the ground where your detector spotted a possible treasure, there is possibility to come across trash. Trash is part of metal detecting and because of that you can get dirty. When you dig out trash during the exercise, do not allow them to litter the environment. You can pack them and drop in a nearby waste basket. Always make our country neat. Be a good citizen.

Importance Notice: Do not go for treasure hunt on any land you are not permitted to do so. Do not think that every land you see is free for you to enter. No land is free. So, ask question before hunting for treasure on any land. Also, obey the law guiding any land you find in any area in the course of metal detecting hobby. Save yourself from paying unnecessary charge due to trespassing.

There is another important message you need to hear. Before you go metal detecting in any location mostly bushy areas, let your loved ones know the direction. There may be dangerous animals in such kind of bush. As a result of that, keep them informed. In addition, arm yourself properly before such movement so that if issue like that arises, you can fight those you have the power to do. I once killed a dangerous snake during a treasure hunt because I had the tool to get the job done on that day. So, be armed always.

Chapter 3

Rules and Getting Permission for Metal Detecting

Any society that is not governed by law and order cannot stand. In that same way, any activity that is not structured with rules may end up making our society disorganized. As a result of that, metal detecting has rules that guides it. That is why the activity is referred to as the most structured in some areas. In this chapter, I will be educating you on the rules of metal detecting.

Also, getting permission before hunting on any land is very important. Such is stressed in United States, United Kingdom and in Australia. If you do not obtain permission before hunting in some lands, you can get fined. It is trespassing. That is not yours and because of that you have to ask before you are given.

Can a detectorist be punished for not observing metal detecting rules?

Yes. Irrespective of how experienced you think you are in metal detecting, if you disobey the rules of metal detecting, you will be punished. The fine you will pay can even be more than the monetary worth of the finds you make.

The Rules of Metal Detecting Explained

The rules of metal detecting are as follow:

Rule number 1: Do not Trespass

Whenever you are out there for metal detecting, do not trespass. If you observe that a particular land is a restricted area, you do not need to break into the land because you want to detect precious metals. If it is boldly written that no one should go inside there and hunt, please respect the instruction of the landowner.

Rule number 2: Do not Hunt in Sensitive Areas

Your life is more important than any kind of treasure. Also, government properties should not be destroyed for no reason even as you make your finds. When you prospect for any kind of treasure, do not hunt along places where pipelines are buried. If it is gas pipelines that pass through the land, hitting them can expose you to danger. Your skin can get burnt or even die in the process. Petroleum is highly flammable so avoid such places. Also, avoid places that electricity wires pass through underground. You can get electrocuted in such area.

Rule Number 3: Stay Clear of National and State Monuments

Do not make the mistake and carry your metal detector close to any national or state monuments including parks. Those areas are protected. In the United States, a national monument is a protected area that is like a national park but can be created from any land owned or controlled by the federal government by proclamation of the President of the United States. Do not allow government to handle your case because you will really sweat.

Rule number 4: Apply reasonable caution in digging toward targets

While you dig targets, make sure you apply proper caution. The reason is because deep seeking machines can detect concealed pipes, wirings and other dangerous materials. When you apply caution as you dig, you can quickly call the attention of the right authority once you notice that.

Rule Number 5: Avoid Military Zones

Please let this last rule enter your skull. Do not make any mistake and hunt in military zones. Do you know if dangerous weapons are buried under the ground? Do you want your body to be damaged by dangerous radiations? I know you will not want that. No matter what you heard on the possible treasures you will find in such locations, do not go there.

How can I get Permission to Detect on A Land?

Getting permission to hunt on lands that do not belong to you is important. That will give you a clear conscience and make you not to fear as you are on the path to your great treasures. In this subheading I will walk you through on how you can get permission to hunt in any location of your choice so far that is not a protected area.

Make Enquiry to locate the Landowner

Property acquisition is expensive. In the other words, buying landed property is expensive. It takes some people long time savings before they owned their land. Putting that into consideration, you have to make enquiry on the owner of the land before going into hunting. If you know the owner in person, you can meet with him or her and let you two discuss. If he says you will give him little of your find after hunting, you can agree with him or her if you are comfortable with that. You can start with the people you know first to those you do not know.

Do not go with Your Machine

You do not need to announce to the public that you are visiting a home because you want to request for them to allow you hunt in their land. Do you know if the neighbor does not like your face and can spoil the mind of the owner when you leave? You are to be wise as you go out there to ask for permission to hunt in any area.

On the other hand, the person you are going to meet may not have full knowledge of metal detector. He may not even allow you to come inside his home because he does not know whether what you are holding is a dangerous weapon. Even if he allows you in, he may not feel comfortable with you and can make him disapprove your request. So, keep your detector at home before going to ask for permission to go metal detecting in a place.

Be Persuasive

Make your discussion with the owner of a property land interactive and be persuasive as you discuss with him or her. Be convincing; act like a marketer. Let him see reasons he needs to let you into his land. You can make him know that life turns around. Tell him that you may end up detecting treasures that will worth thousands of dollars and he, the own, will still gain from it.

Stick to the Agreement

If at the beginning you reached an agreement with the owner, make sure you fulfill it. If you agreed with him that you will fill all holes after digging, do that diligently. If you also agreed with him that you will give him few finds, still do that. Sticking to the agreement can make him give you another good site to go hunt for valuable metals.

Chapter 4

Mastering Your Metal Detector

If you do not master how to use your metal detector, you will find it difficult to make good finds. This is the reason you are to understand this chapter. The good end product of every metal detecting outing is treasure which can be Gold, Silver, coins, artifacts, jewelries or any other valuable finds. In respect to this, no matter how expensive a metal detector is, if it does not make any find, it is equal to having less sensitive metal detector. Because the sound end product is important to us, I have to properly do justice to this chapter.

Because this teaching is on metal detector and other important parts of the machine, I will discuss some other basic parts I explained before. It will make you to really understand the teaching. Without metal detector, there will be nothing like metal detecting hobby of the modern time. So, let us keep the ball rolling.

Search coil

The search coil is the engine house of every metal detector. If there is no search coil in a metal detector, there is no way the metal detector can communicate with the target. The search coil section is the center of communication between targets and a metal detector.

A search coil is coil of wires located at the end of a metal detector which is used to detect targets. It is these rounds of wires that make metal detecting possible. The coils that make a metal detector can be small or big in size. Many metal detector enthusiasts prefer small coils to large coils, but all of them have their strengths and weaknesses.

Search coil which is built with small coils are very sensitive than large coil in terms of target detection. But when the target is hidden inside dirt, it becomes a problem to this kind of search coil, and hence large coils is the best in that situation. It is recommended you have metal detectors which are built with small and large coils. This will make it easy for you to switch depending on where you find yourself.

The 8 inches coil is all purpose coil which is the most popular coil in metal detecting. In Gold prospecting, the 10inches by 5inches coils are good for finding small Gold.

Audio Tone

When you grow to certain stage in the field of metal detecting, you will begin to notice some things about the tones of different type of metals. Metal detecting is like a school where you learn some basic ideas as you grow in the field. There will be a stage you will get to know the sound of Gold, Silver, Iron and even Steel when your detector sense them under the ground. When you get to that professional level, you do not have to dig everything you come across. But as a beginner, you have to do that at this state.

In general, when your search coil detects nonferrous metals, it gives medium to high tone. This is how detectors in general are built. In metallurgy, a non-ferrous metal is a metal, including alloys, that does not contain iron in appreciable amounts. Examples of nonferrous metals are Gold, Silver and Copper.

When your metal detector comes across ferrous metals, it gives low audio tone. As a result of this, you are to develop good listening habit as you hunt for treasures in different locations. Common examples of ferrous metals are iron and steel. Some artifacts are made with steel and metal detector can find them and give low tone in return.

Target indicator

The target indicator of a metal detector simply shows which metal is detected by the machine. If it is gold, that is shown on the target indicator of the machine.

Target ID Number

With this feature available in the modern-day metal detectors, you can see the numbers of targets that have been detected on the screen of your machine. This range of the numbers vary depending on the manufacturer. In some are from –4 to 44 on the X-Terra 305 and –9 to 48 on the X-Terra 505. Negative numbers represent ferrous targets and positive numbers represent nonferrous targets.

Depth Indicator

Depth indicator in metal detecting machines is a welcomed development. With this property, metal detector informs you how deep a target is beneath the ground before digging. The depth can be shallow, medium or very deep. It prepares you on how much energy you are to spend before you get to your treasure. Depth indicator shows on the screen of some metal detectors.

Magnetic Mineralization Intensity

This property available in some metal detectors informs the user of the intensity of mineral under a ground. This goes a long way in making users select the suitable metal detectors for a particular environment. Example of a detector that has this property is Nokta Makro Gold Metal Detector.

Assembling and Understanding Your Metal Detector

The first thing to do after you bought your metal detector is to open and assemble it. Metal detector is made up of many parts including search coil, control box, shaft, and handle. The different parts of a metal detector are assembled to form a unit at the end.

When you open the package of your metal detector as it arrives, the first thing to get from the package is the manual. Through the manual, you will be guided on how to set the machine up. Many metal detectors come with battery to power the machine, but if that is lacking in your own, you can buy the appropriate ones needed for your own machine.

After assembling your metal detector, the next thing to do is to study the behavior of your machine in respect to different metal types. By that, I mean the audio your metal detector will give per metal type. For example, the audio for Gold cannot be the same for Iron.

So, to find out the audio that is unique to any kind of metal, bury different metal types in different spots in your environment. Sweep your detector through each of those metals to find out the sound unique to each. With time, you will begin to master your machine.

Is it Right to Change My Metal Detector Frequently?

The answer is NO. If your metal detector is bad and does not give you the accuracy you desire during prospecting of treasures, you can change it. But if the one you have is still sound, you do not need frequent change. Having your one metal detector which is suitable for detecting on a particular kind of environment is okay. This will make you to master and even "marry" your detector.

Troubleshooting in Metal Detector

Troubleshooting is a way of getting solution to the challenge encountered while trying to complete a particular task. When you go out for treasure hunt, there may come to a time when your machine stops to work. At that point, you may end up feeling angry. The troubleshooting measures to quickly take are as follow:

1. You are to check the battery section of your machine to find out if positioned properly when your detector refuses to turn on.
2. Clean the metal detector battery terminals with clean dry cloth.
3. When your metal detector refuses to turn on, quickly change the batteries as that may be the reason for the challenge.
4. If your metal detector screen shows **OL** on the screen which stands for **Overload**, check to see if your search coil is facing a large metal and remove it from there
5. If you notice problem in the depth of detection in your detector, just check the settings of your machine and fix it.
6. If your search coil section is loose, tight the plastic bolts but if it does not fix the problem, just change the washers.

The Impacts of Minerals on Metal Detectors

As a beginner, I want you to know that all metal detectors are not suitable for all kind of grounds. There are some minerals that prevent "ordinary" metal detectors from discovering some metals in the ground. A mineral is a naturally occurring crystalline solid that cannot be physically broken down into smaller components. Some of the natural occurring minerals like irons, salt and hematite can affect your metal detector for going deep in the ground to detect a treasure. If you want to hunt for treasures on mineralized ground, one of the best metal detectors to get the job in that area done is called ground balance metal detector.

Chapter 5

Classifications of Metal Detectors

Irrespective of the three basic types of metal detectors based on technology involved, there are other classifications of metal detectors. These classifications are based on the manufacturer and their applications to certain metals detection and environment. In this chapter, I will walk you through on these metal detectors, and what some of them are best at. After going through this chapter, it will guide you to make the best choice during metal detectors selection. Let us get started.

Minelab Metal Detectors

Minelab metal detectors are my best as a professional treasure hunter. They give me all the result I need at a point in time when I want to switch to a different mode while searching for treasures. Minelab metal detectors are excellent detectors when it comes to Gold prospecting. They can detect Gold easily when the search coil runs over the metal.

Another good thing about this kind of metal detector is the ability to go deep into the group. Detectors made by Minelab can go deep into the ground through the search coils and give signal in return on what was detected. You can turn on the discrimination mode to separate the trash from the valuable as you search.

With this kind of metal detector, you can switch search coils depending on the environment you want to prospect on. If you want a large coil, you can switch and vice versa. The company makes the machine flexible. Minelab metal detectors are produced by a company called Minelab. You can access their website through www.minelab.com.

Fig 5: Equinox 800 Minelab metal detector

There are many types of minelab metal detectors. These metal detectors include:

1. Minelab X-Terra 705
2. GPZ 7000

3. CTX 3030
4. X-TERRA 705 Dual and Gold pack
5. X-Terra 505
6. X-Terra 303
7. Vanquish 340
8. Vanquish 440
9. Vanquish 540
10. Equinox 800
11. Equinox 600
12. E-Trac
13. Safari and many others

All Minelab metal detectors are built with sophisticated technologies to adapt in many ground conditions and make finds. Equinox 800 Minelab metal detector for instance has four major modes you can switch to depending on your ground type and target. These modes are Park, Field, Beach and Gold. Minelab metal detectors are durable.

Bounty Hunter Metal Detectors

Bounty Hunter metal detectors are simple and affordable metal detectors which operate with Very Low Frequency (VLF) technology system. These metal detectors are what many professional treasure hunters we have in our society today started with. Irrespective of the simplicity of the metal detector, it comes with the basic tools expected from a standard metal detector.

Metal detectors of this type have discrimination property. With the discrimination dial, you can separate trash from the valuable metals as you progress in your metal detecting. This gives you the opportunity to detect value rather than trash in the form of pieces of lead.

Bounty Hunter metal detector has **Sensitivity** button at the control box. With this property, you can increase the sensitivity of the detector as you prospect for treasures. If the **Sensitivity** is turned higher, the measure the search coil will go into the ground becomes increased. That is to say that the detector will have high depth of detection.

Warranty is a way of maintaining good business relationship between companies and customers. It is an important area to put into consideration when selling electronic products to people. Bounty Hunter metal detectors come with warranty. If your newly bought Bounty Hunter metal detector develops fault within the warranty period, you can take it back to the seller to be fixed or replaced depending on the level of the damage.

In addition, Bounty Hunter metal detectors are good for children. The company produces many metal detectors geared toward use by the teenagers in the society. I remember getting one for my son some time ago. He liked it and made some good finds with it. One of the things I like about the detector is its lightness. It is easy to carry about by children.

Metal detectors of this class are adjustable. You can adjust them to the length you want them. Maybe someone else wants to make use of it and he does not like its adjustment level at that point, he can easily make a change that will suit him.

One of the challenges in most Bounty Hunter metal detectors is their inability to detect treasures in mineralized area. That is a weakness and it is so because of the technology the metal detectors are built on. Bounty Hunter metal detectors work with VLF technology.

Bounty Hunter metal detectors are many in the market today. The models are much including the following:

1. Fast track metal detector
2. Tracker II metal detector
3. Tracker IV metal detector and
4. Bounty Hunter pioneer EX metal detector

You can access more Bounty Hunter metal detectors through her website www.detecting.com.

Bounty Hunter Pioneer EX Metal Detector

I want to explain more on this class of Bounty Hunter metal detector because I like its feature. Bounty Hunter pioneer EX metal detector is light and good at gold detecting. It is adjustable and can be used by both children and adults to hunt for treasures. It is produced in United States of America. When ordered, the product comes with 5 years warranty.

The control box of the machine houses all the electronics. This includes discrimination, sensitivity and other properties involving electronics. When using this device, ensure you shield the box from wet environment to avoid damage. This machine works with two 9-volt batteries. These batteries must be alkaline batteries for the machine to function well.

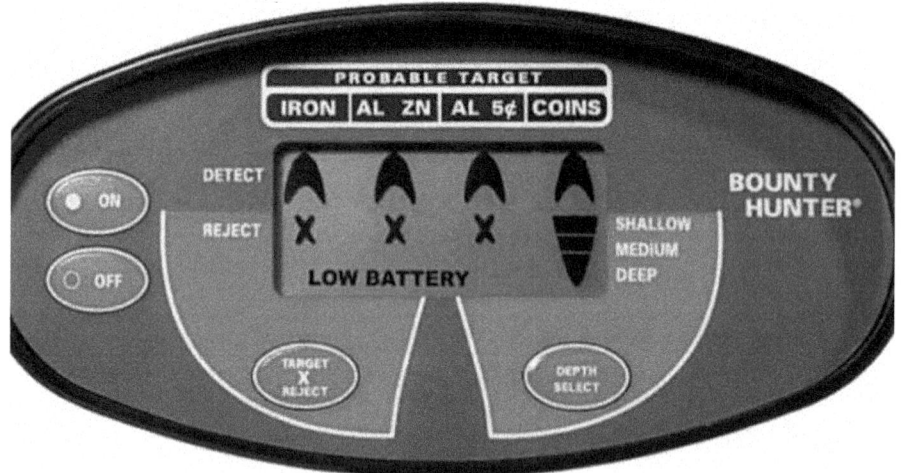

Fig 5.1: The control box of Bounty Hunter Pioneer EX metal detector

With the **Depth Select** touchpad on the control box of the machine, you can change the depth rate of the detector to detect into the ground. Also, the depth select touchpad is used to reduce electromagnetic interference on the metal detector.

This metal detector can target metals made of Iron, Aluminum, Zinc, Gold, and coins. When target is detected while searching, the machine gives audible sound. There are three major audio sounds in Bounty Hunter Pioneer EX metal detector but one is given at a point.

With **TARGET REJECT** touchpad, you can reject any metal you do not want when your detector comes across any. It makes your work less stressful and saves you from wasting your time on unwanted metals.

Teknetics Metal Detectors

This is a good beginner's kind of metal detector. It is simple to operate and carry about. There are many good features integrated into this metal detector which makes it suitable for use in different locations.

The Teknetics metal detectors are manufactured by a company named First Texas Products. This company is in the United States of America. They are the manufacturer of Bounty Hunter metal detectors as well as Fisher Labs metal detectors.

Can Teknetics metal detectors find Gold?

Yes. Teknetics metal detectors can find Gold. Irrespective of the small price tag of the machine, it can still detect Gold when hunting with it.

Is Teknetics metal detectors good for beginners?

Yes. This metal detector is good for beginners. In fact, it is one of the best for beginners due to its simplicity.

You can visit the company website at https://www.tekneticsdirect.com and get any metal detector of your choice.

Fisher Lab Metal Detectors

Fisher Lab metal detectors are produced by First Texas Products Company as stated before now. Their metal detectors are light and simple to operate as well. Under Fisher Lab metal detectors, there are those designed for multipurpose metal treasure detecting. Example of such machines are Fisher F44 Visual & Audio Target ID Metal Detector, Fisher F22 Visual & Audio Target ID Metal Detector, Fisher F11 Visual & Audio Target ID Metal Detector, Fisher F2 Visual & Audio Target ID Metal Detector and Fisher F4 Visual & Audio Target ID Metal Detector. These metal detectors are good at detecting coins, jewelries and relics.

Fisher Lab metal detectors are built with sound sensitivity and discrimination tones. The tones produced by the machines vary depending on the metal detected. There are specific metal detectors produced by the company to detect mainly Gold. These metal detectors are Fisher Gold Bug-2 Metal Detector and Fisher Gold Bug Metal Detector. The detectors function with 2 Search Modes: All Metal and Discriminate. Also, when you buy them, they come with manual to guide you through.

You can have access to the gallery of Fisher Lab metal detectors by visiting their website via http://www.fisherlab.com.

Garrett Metal Detectors

Garrett metal detectors are simple and good detectors for beginners. They are built with sound features. The touchpad on the control box is used to set the detector functions before and during detecting. You can control the sensitivity and discrimination modes of the machine through that place. The detectors of this class have adjustable arm strap and cuff. The machines come with manual to guide you assemble it.

There are many Garrett detectors in the market. These include Garrett apex metal detector, Garrett ACE 250, Garrett AT Gold, Garrett AT Pro metal detectors, and Garrett ACE 350 metal detector which are few among the many.

Some Garrett metal detectors have waterproof control boxes. Examples of such metal detector are Garret AT Gold and Garrett AT MAX.

To access many Garrett detectors, visit the company website at https://garrett.com.

Garrett ACE 250 Metal Detectors

Garrett ACE 250 is a nice machine and it weighs about 2.7bls. It has a waterproof search coil part. The metals that can be detected by this machine include coins, jewelry, Gold, Silver, relics and so on .Garrett

ACE 250 metal detector works with headphones but I advise you buy another one that will give you increased volume the way you want it.

The machine has proven to be a great metal detector for beginners. It is strong, simple to use and very affordable.

Hunting with Garrett ACE 250 Metal Detector as a Beginner

When you want to hunt with this kind of machine as a beginner, I advise you start with sandy environment. You can start with beach treasure hunt exercise. This is because hunting on that kind of place is easy. It will also help you understand how the detector works for best result.

Garrett ACE 250 is a good metal detector and you will enjoy it once you master how to operate it.

Chapter 6

Safety and Relics Metal Detecting

The saying "safety first" are not new words. If they are new to you, I have been hearing that since my high school days till now. Safety is very important. It will be a stupid act for a metal detecting hobbyist to make great finds and ends up not spending the money he made from the finds because of poor safely measure. Because of how important safety is in metal detecting, I will discuss that in this chapter. That will help you to know what you must do before and during treasure hunt.

Relics are important treasures. Relics can be defined in this context as objects surviving from an earlier time, especially one of historical interest. Museums cherish relics and can pay good amount of money to have them. They have cultural values.

There are some relics which were made from expensive Gold and today are not found due to the impact of wars in such locations. Some of them are of royal importance. Imagine finding such relics that contains high quantity of Gold? Even if museums do not pay good amount of money, individuals and companies can buy and use it to reproduce other metal objects that can give them more money in return.

In this book chapter, I will also cover relics finding. I will walk you through on the best metal detectors you can use for your hunt of relics.

Safety Precautions in Metal Detecting

The following are the safety measures you are to take during metal detecting

1. Wear the right clothes

It is important you wear the right clothing to protect yourself whenever you are going out for metal detecting. The environment you are going determines whether you wear light or thick clothes. Also, you must wear the right shoes or safety boots. Do not think you are just going out there to play; so, protect yourself properly. Also, check the weather report for the day. It will help you know the environmental weather for the day and hence guide with your dressing.

2. Be conscious of Sunlight

Many metal detecting enthusiasts are less concerned of this. I want to bring to your notice that the rate of skin cancer in our society today is high. And the cancer is caused by Ultraviolet rays from the sun. So, you can check the weather report of the area you are prospecting to hunt for treasure to find out how sunny the location will be.

Also, you are to wear your sunshield glasses as you progress into hunting of treasures. If you do not have any, try and get one for yourself. Protect your eyes because they are important.

3. Go with Knives

You must arm yourself as you hunt for valuable treasures in some areas. You do not know if there is dangerous animal in that bush you want to go in and hunt. Because of that, you are to go with sharp knives as a precautionary measure.

4. Have first aid materials with you

You never thought of sustaining injury as you hunt for treasures before? It does happen and because of that you have to be ready at all time. I know of a friend that mistakenly hit shovel on his leg when he was digging for treasure. If such incidence happens to you and you have first aid materials in your bag, you can give yourself treatment that will sustain you until you finish your hunting.

5. Maintain good communication with people

As you go for metal detecting hunt, go with your mobile phone. Always communicate with your loved ones concerning your locations and your where about. It will make it easy for you to be reached in any emerged.

6. Go with map to hunt for treasures

Irrespective of the fact that our electronic device, example phone can help us with the location we want to go and hunt for treasures, it is not enough. Such electronics device has failed in some cases. As a result of this challenge, please go with physical map that will guide you to the environment you want to hunt for treasures. The map will lead you to your destination and help you find your way back.

Relic Metal Detectors

If your target is to find relics which are lost in any environment for many years now, then you need relic metal detector to get the job done. In the absence of a metal detector designed to find relics, you can use multipurpose metal detector and set it in relic mode through the control box.

Relic metal detectors can easily detect metals which are made of Iron, Steel and Brass. Many relics of historical values are usually made from any of these types of metals. First is to make your decision on the environment you want to search for the relic treasures and the second is choosing the best machine for the job. Metal detectors with low frequency are best for unearthing relics.

Some metal detectors that can detect relics are as follow:

- Bounty Hunter Platinum metal detector
- Fisher F5 metal detector
- Garrett ATX metal detector
- XP DEUS Wireless Metal Detector
- Minelab CTX 3030
- Teknetics T2 Special Limited Edition

- Garrett ACE 400
- Nokta Makro Invenio and
- Whites MX Sport

From the above list of metal detectors, you can choose any for relic metal detecting. As I explained that relics are detected at low frequency, you can reduce the frequency of your detector as you make your find.

Garrett ACE 400 for Relics Metal Detecting

Garrett ACE 400 is a modern-day Garrett Metal Detector. The machine is built with advanced features and that is why it has the capacity to detect relics. The features of this machine include Iron Audio, Digital Target ID, and Frequency Adjust.

With the **Frequency Adjust** property, it can help you dig more treasure and less trash. Also, this property makes it possible for you to reduce the frequency to be able to detect relics. Relics detecting is more at low frequency.

Chapter 7

Coin Shooting and Metal Detectors for Other Areas

The term "coin shooting" is the process of searching for old coins using the appropriate metal detecting machine. I remember the first time I embarked on coin detecting. It was not easy because I searched at length before I could make a find. But do you know what? When I uncovered an ancient Roman coin at a point, I was very excited. The excitement got me addicted to shooting of coins. I love such hobby. An old valued coin you may uncover can worth up to a thousand dollars.

You have to understand your metal detector to succeed in coin shooting. Your metal detector has to be set in a way that it can discriminate Iron. The target is usually Silver. When you uncover old Silver coins that are over 150 years ago, you will smile. You will smile because you know you have lay your hands on valuable treasure.

There are metal detectors that work best in coins shooting. These machines were produced by manufacturers to give coin shooters the best result. Also, there are some multipurpose metal detectors that can perform the same function. In these metal detectors, all you have to do is to give it the needed settings to detect coins through the control box and you are good to go.

Metal Detectors for Coins Shooting

The metal detectors suitable for coins shooting are as follow:

1. Garrett ACE metal detectors
2. Bounty Hunter Gold
3. Whites CoinMaster
4. Fisher F4
5. Garrett AT Pro
6. Fisher F70
7. Whites MX Sport and
8. Nokta Makro Anfibio Multi

Tips in Coin Shooting and Coins Maintenance

As an experienced metal detecting hobbyist, I have to teach you something I know about this areas of the greatest hobby in the world. There are some ideas you need to have before you go deep into coin shooting. These tips are as follow:

1. When you dig out a coin from a spot, do not be in a hurry to go because there may be cluster of coins within the same environment. So, still take your time to check around there.

2. Dig slowly and carefully. When your metal detector detects coins, slowly and carefully dig the spot so that you do not damage the coins. Give good allowance while digging.
3. Do not clean your coins too much. If you clean it too much with strong or hard object, you may end up damaging the surface of the coins. It is better you wash with water or leave it in a semi-crude state until you get to the buyer.
4. Make use of pinpointer which is also known as probe to guide you to the exact spot where the coins are in the hole you dig. Coins are small and because of that you need this device to make your focus at a particular locality.
5. For effective result, you have to set your metal detector to discriminate other metals except coins before coin shooting. Let your detector be set at coins mode.

Where can I go to coin shooting?
There are many places you can go and discover coins including:

1. Homes that were abandoned long years ago
2. Areas that experienced wars long years ago like World War 1 and 2 arears
3. Parks
4. Rivers (only go if you have experience in swimming)
5. Beaches
6. Back yards and
7. Ball fields

Underwater Metal Detecting

One common thing about underwater metal detectors is that they have waterproof search coil. They are designed that way so that they do not get damaged.

When the machine sweeps over a metal as you are inside water, it beeps. Through the audible sound, you can use your hand scoop to gather the white sand around it and retrieve the treasure from it. Sometimes, you have to use your hand pinpointer to trace the close location to the target. The pinpointers used for underwater metal detecting are also waterproof. Please know that before you go into underwater metal detecting, you must know how to swim, and also dress the right way.

Do not take your average entry level metal detector into river, ocean or lake for treasure hunt because it will not give you the expected result. Underwater metal detectors are waterproof detectors and they can withstand pressure. So, take these points into consideration.

Underwater Metal Detectors

There are many good underwater metal detectors. These detectors include the following:

1. Minelab Excalibur II
2. Bounty Hunter Tk4 Tracker underwater metal detector
3. Garrett at prounder water metal detector and

4. Minelab equinox 600 multi IQ underwater metal detector

These underwater metal detectors are completely submersible machines. When you work with them, they provide you with maximum output through minimum effort. They are multi-frequency metal detectors. They have the capacity to go deep under the water. They can be used in river, lake or ocean.

Other underwater metal detectors that work greatly are:

- Kkmoon underwater metal detector

This machine functions with pulse induction technology. It can detect treasures at 30 meters deep in water. It is suitable for treasure hunt in both fresh and salt waters.

- RM RICOMAX underwater and
- Kuman automatic underground metal detector

All these machines come with manual on how to assemble and use them.

Minelab Excalibur II Underwater Metal Detector

Minelab is known as one of the best metal detectors manufacturers. Their products are of good quality and they showed that through their Excalibur II metal detector. This machine is considered the best in underwater produced by the company as of the time of first publication of this book. It is a clear representation of technology advancement in the field of metal detector.

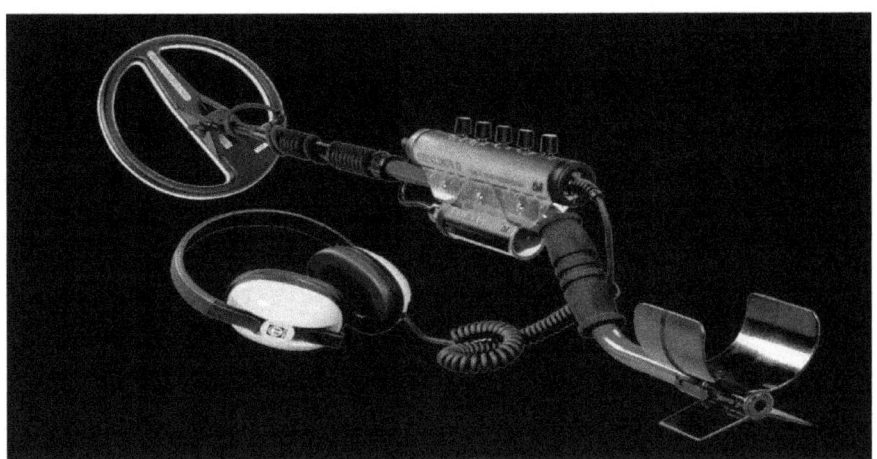

Fig 7: Excalibur II metal detector

The machine shows extreme underwater performance. It works with multi-frequency BBS technology. It is waterproof for up to 200ft (66m). It comes with slimline 10" coil. It is not that heavy and has improved balance.

In terms of technology, the machine functions with Broad Band Spectrum (BBS) of between 1.5 kHz — 25.5 kHz. Excalibur II metal detector functions with rechargeable battery which can sustain the detector for straight 12 hours once fully charged. If you are a diver that detects underwater, you can go for it.

Gold Detecting
Gold is usually the main target of every beginner in metal detecting. Gold is a precious metal and every individual wants to lay their hands on it. It can occur in lumps or in pieces. Some jewelries are made of gold and when lost, and later discovered by a metal detecting

enthusiast, can be a good source of money to him or her. In metal detecting jargon, Gold is referred to as **color**. Pure Gold is slightly reddish yellow in color, but colored Gold in various other colors can be produced.

Where can Gold be detected?

In metal detecting, there are places where Gold can be detected. The places are as follow:

1. River
2. In waterways
3. Ocean
4. Rocky areas and
5. In gold mining sites

Metal Detectors for Gold Detecting

Though virtually all metal detectors can find Gold, there are some that do better. These are metal detectors manufactured for the main purpose of Gold metal detection. Though some of these machines can be expensive, but they worth the money if you can utilize them effectively.

The following metal detectors are good for Gold finding and I have made use of them to discover quality finds:

1. **Gold Monster 1000**: It operates automatically in an easy-to-use way. It is high performance detector with automatic noise cancel, automatic ground balance and automatic sensitivity.
2. **GPX-4500**: This is a Minelab Gold metal detector which has the capacity to detect gold of different sizes. It is built with sophisticated technology and can penetrate deep into mineralized ground more than many Pulse Induction metal detectors. It has six search modes which you can modified with your favorite settings and can rename them.
3. **X-Terra705 Gold Pack metal detector**: This is another Gold prospecting metal detector which uses VFLEX technology with an accurate preset Prospecting Mode. This makes it the ideal entry level gold detector. I know you may be worried on what VFLEX is all about. VFLEX provides increased detecting performance with perfect sine wave transmission, an in-coil signal booster and coil selectable transmit frequencies.

The other Gold metal detectors you can buy for your Gold prospecting are

4. **Whites Goldmaster GMT** and
5. **Fisher Gold Bug 2**

Metal Detectors for Kids

That statement "experience is the best teacher" is true and practical. If you have already started metal detecting hobby and you like what you do, you will like to teach the young. If you have children, you will like to teach them how to start prospecting for treasures even when they are still young. If you start teaching your children metal detecting hobby at young age, they are likely to become experts when they grow to adulthood.

I have experience in metal detecting because I was carried along when I was still a teenager. In this section, you will learn metal detecting for kids. You can get any of the metal detectors for any kid you want to learn along with you. Without taking much time, metal detecting for kids are as follow:

1. Garrett ACE 300
2. Fisher F4
3. Bounty Hunter Junior T. I. D
4. Bounty Hunter Tracker IV and
5. Fisher F22

Multipurpose Metal Detectors

As a beginner, you are likely to be passionate to lay your hands on any kind of metal treasure. Be it Gold, relics, Silver, coins or jewelries, you want to have your hands on any. If you feel like this, then you need multipurpose metal detector. The configurations of these types of metal detectors can vary. In some metal detectors of this type, you have to set the machine to **All metal** mode so as to detect any metal it comes across.

On the other hand, you can choose to select any metal you want to hunt for through the control box of the machine.

Examples of multipurpose metal detectors are:

1. Fisher 70 multi-purpose metal detector
2. Garrett ACE 150 metal detector
3. Bounty Hunter TK4 Tracker IV metal detector
4. XP Deus Wireless metal detector and others

Chapter 8

Detecting in Water, Treasure Identification and Other Teachings

Water which includes rivers, oceans and lakes house many treasures. The treasures which can be found under water cuts across Gold, Silver, and relics. Rivers, oceans and lakes house many uncovered treasures. It is not every metal detecting hobbyist can hunt in such places and because of that still have many untapped treasures till date.

If for instance you want to hunt in ocean, you must first know how to dive or swim very well. If you do not have the qualities of a diver, that has first disqualified you to hunt in such location. So, the number of metal detecting enthusiasts likely to hunt in the ocean has reduced. There are many relics which were lost by travelers long years ago because their boat capsized. Who is going to discover these relics and make money from them one day?

What are the possible Treasures to be discovered in Rivers and Oceans?

The possible finds from River and oceans are:

1. Gold
2. Old coins
3. Silver
4. Relics
5. Rings and
6. Jewelries

While searching in river, if your target is to detect gold, then prospect areas of the river where there is outcropping of gold bearing quartz rock. You stand a high chance to find such metal in that location than any other part of the river. The Gold may be small. Irrespective of the size, it is still a material of great value. You can scoop the sand of the river and use your detector to prospect for Gold exact spot.

Metal Detecting in Beach

I will like you to learn something interesting in this subheading. The reason is because I do not feel good to see beginners in this precious exercise suffer themselves much in the name of trying to find treasures on the beach. It can be painful to dig large hole on beach ground in the name you are getting signal. That signal may be bad signal because of the nature of the environment you are metal detecting.

Before you go into detecting in a beach, there are some questions you have to ask yourself first; what kind of water is the beach am planning to go metal detecting? Is it a salt or fresh water? What metal detector can work best in that water to give me the best result I need? Is my metal detector made for wet ground or not? These are the questions you need to ask and answer yourself before you go metal detecting in any beach.

I some time ago came across one young man who was digging serious hole on a beach ground in the name that he was getting a signal for possible treasure. When I got to the spot where he was busy stressing himself, I just stood by. I politely asked why digging such deep hole, he answered he was getting signal that his metal detector was beeping at that spot.

I gently picked up the detector and looked at it. I found out the detector was not made for such environment. I smiled within myself because I knew the young man was busy getting bad signals. I told him that there was no treasure in where he was digging. I explained further to him that he was getting bad signals because the detector was not meant for saltwater beach. I later gave him the name of an entry-level metal detector he can go get for himself for such kind of beach. Very Low Frequency metal detectors (VLF) that have ground adjust control can take care of the salt beach detecting challenge. With this feature, you can turn your machine to the level of mineralization you want. But at best, pulse induction metal detectors do the job neatly.

Some saltwater beaches are high in minerals. As a result of this, your detector will be affected if you do not employ the right one. So, put this into consideration before going into any beach to hunt for treasures. It is very important to know that.

Beach Metal Detectors

The following are sound metal detectors you can buy for beach hunting for treasures:

1. Whites TDI BeachHunter metal detector
2. White's Spectra V3i HP metal detector
3. Garrett Sea Hunter Mark II Underwater metal detector with 2 Search Coils
4. Bounty Hunter Platinum metal detector
5. Garrett ATX metal detector and
6. Makro Multi-Kruzer metal detector

Identifying Your Finds with Metal Detector Feature

With the new technology development in metal detecting hobby, you can know what your metal detector detects before unearthing to bring out the find. It is a welcomed idea and makes detecting treasures easy for us. When I first handled this kind of metal detector, I was amazed but today it is a normal thing as many other technologies are evolving.

With a technology called **target identification indicator** which informs you of the possible find under the ground, you will know the kind of find your detector gets across to. It can be Gold, Silver, bronze or artifacts. This information is displayed in the LCD of your metal detector screen. Another way you can also identify the find is through the signal given by the detector.

Explaining further on target ID, different metal is represented with different target ID number. Also, the target ID that explains any particular metal detected vary per metal detector manufacturer. With my Teknetics metal detector, whenever it shows target ID number of 88 when am hunting for treasures, it is likely to be a Silver dime. Also, other metals have their own unique number.

You do not need to worry much about target identification indicator of the metals that are represented on the screen of your own metal detector. The reason is because it is explained in the manual of your own detector. Read through your machine manual and you will see the target indicator code for each metal that will be detected by your machine. The introduction of target identification indicator in metal detectors have saved us from digging anything shown on the screen as possible valuable metals while they are not.

Some metal detectors instead of using the term target identification indicator work with **Visual Display Indication (VDI)** but all still convey the same message. They are all ways to know the possible metal found before digging. Whites detectors make use of the term Visual Display Indication.

As a beginner in metal detecting hobby, I will advise you dig everything at first. When you master your detector over the years, you can then start following target ID and VDI including the use of discrimination modes. It is one step at a time.

Guide on Identifying Your Coins

Coins are treasures which are valued in treasure hunt. The price for coins varies. Some are sold at high cost while some lower. Coins dealers value coins differently. In this heading, I will be teaching you how you can know the value of your coins by identifying them. If you detected a coin during treasure hunt and want to identify it by knowing how old the coins is, the place of origin, the value or even know the monetary worth, take these steps:

• Find the denomination of the coins

• Discover the date of the coins as well as the shape

• Understand the size of the coins and take measurement of their diameters

• Distinguish the colors of the coins

• Properly understand the language on the coins because it can make you know the possible country of production of the coins.

• Download and install coin checking application in your phone to check the information about the coins. If you make use of Android phone, you can download and install from Playstore. If you make use of iOS phones, just download and install from App Store. Just search for coin checker and you will be shown many of them. If you are in United States, you can download and install the one called U.S Coin Checker.

• Post photos of your found coins in forums of metal detecting hobbyists as a member may have information of the coins.

• Send email showing the image of the coins to coin dealers. They will identify the treasure and give you feedback.

• You can use search engine example Google to make research of the image on the coins. Wikipedia may have written article about the same images. If Wikipedia does not have any article on that, another blogger may have something on it.

How to identify Relics
You may dig out relics that command cultural respect but do not know what it really is. It may look odd, but it is valued by people. Identifying the age by yourself may be a difficult task. To confirm its really relics or artifacts you found, just look for archeologists. They will tell you better.

How to identify Jewelries
I know that when you see jewelries like rings, necklaces, and bracelets that you can easily identify them. That will not be any problem to you for sure. But where the problem lies is knowing the one that is pure

and original. If they are jewelries with hullmark, you can easily identify them. In the absent of that, just meet jeweler to confirm the authenticity.

Accessories Needed for Metal Detecting

If you want to be a successful metal detecting hobbyist, then you are to equip yourself with the right tools. Getting the right tools is more than just having a metal detector. You need backup as you embark on the journey. I will walk you through on these important accessories you need to go hunting with.

Metal detector Bags

Metal detector bag is needed in metal detecting. It is a very essential accessory. When going for hunt, make sure you go with it. With the bag, you will put the treasures you will find inside and put other important tools you will be going with as well.

A Pinpointer

A pinpointer is a handheld metal detecting device. It leads you to the close direction of where a target you are searching for is located. Where a metal detector cannot reach, a pinpointer goes there. It has wand-shape and that is what makes it possible. It is also known as probe. A pinpointer is like a touch which leads detectorists to close path of any target. Some pinpointers are waterproof while others are not. Pinpointers can be bought from metal detector dealers or even from Amazon.

Apron and safety Boots

Getting dirty while unearthing treasures is normal but hanging apron round your neck can minimize it. You can go with apron into metal detecting field. Also, going with extra pair of safety boot in your bag is not something bad. This will keep your feet safe from any form of injury should the one you wear gets damaged.

Batteries

If your metal detector batteries have failed you one day, that is when you will understand the importance of going detecting with extra batteries. Do not go to any metal detecting outing without having spare batteries with you. That batteries inside your machine can get weak at any time. If your batteries run down in an environment where there is no shop around to buy and replace it immediately, you will regret that day. Take this advice, DO NOT GO OUT FOR METAL DETECTING WITHOUT EXTRA BATTERIES WITH YOU. Go with the ones that are suitable to your metal detector.

Shovel

There is no form of metal detecting that does not involve digging of holes. Because you must dig holes, you need to go with your sharp shovel. Also, shovel is an important tool for relics hunting due to the fact that most relics are buried deeply in ground. You can buy metal detecting shovel from any dealer close to you. They are many so you have your choice to make on the one that will be okay for you.

Headphones

Many metal detectors come with headphones. Headphones are important components of the modern-day metal detector. When you wear headphone while prospecting any metal treasure, you can hear audios clearly. This is different from when you use speaker of the machine which you are like to miss any target with. Headphone gives the tone closer into your ear. In this situation, you can hear even very low tone produced by the machine which can be due to the tiny size of the target.

Digger

You may meet hardly packed sand as you go on with your treasure hunt. Because of this, you need a sizeable digger. It will help you make the sand lose and you proceed and pick your treasure.

Pouch

This is the tool you need to put all your metal detecting finds in. It is a tool for optimum security of your treasures. Some detectorists have a favorite pouch they make use of, but you can get yourself any.

How to recover a Target

If you do not learn the way to recover your target when detected by a metal detector, you will end up making a mistake. You may scratch the surface of your treasure or even damage it completely.

To recover your target in good condition, adhere to these instructions:

1. When your detector finds the treasure, as you dig a hole, cut a c-shape to a half circle and dig instead of digging the whole areas. As you dig the hole, if any object blocks the way, remove it with your shovel and keep going.

2. Retrieve your treasure with your hands when you get to it. But if you notice it is still far, use pinpointer to find out the exact path of the treasure until you get to it.

3. When you retrieve your treasure at the end, ensure you cover the hole back with the sand you dug out. Also, step on it so that the ground looks neat again.

Making Good Research before Treasure Hunt Outing

At professional level, you cannot just go out for treasure hunting without first making proper research on the area you want to go for your metal detecting. I want you to start practicing that on time because it will make you a professional on time.

In this context, the word "research" implies a systematic investigation over an area. I will walk you through on how to make this research. To make the research, take the follow these steps:

Identify the Place you want to hunt

You have to identify the place or environment you want to go for your metal detecting first. The place can be an abandoned home, old war area or environment covered with rocks.

Use library to find more Information about the place

It is true that wisdom is buried in books. When you read good books, you gain knowledge that will help in one or two places. So, going to library is a way forward to gain knowledge on the area you want to go and hunt.

You can tell the library official in charge of sorting out books to help you get a book about a particular area of interest. This will give you the information that is basic. At the end of reading through the book, you will find out the possible treasures accessible through that location. This will help you make decision on whether to go hunting there or not.

You can take note and get permission

When you make your research, you can take note so as not to forget any important point that will help your hunting. Pen down some important points about the location. At the end, get permission from the management of the environment and proceed with your hunting.

Locate the main target area

Since you have finally gotten information about the area from the library, you can now determine the target area you want to detect on. You can use area map to get the job done. At the end, you will find yourself in the main target location for your "treasures harvesting".

Chapter 9

Enhancing Your Detecting Skill, Cleaning and Selling Your Finds

In life, we improve in our individual skills as we continue to work in a particular area of importance. The same thing applies in metal detecting hobby. You improve as you practice and learn something new in the field.

In this chapter, I will walk you through on what you are to do to improve your skill. You need to learn from other experts to grow. If you want to see far as a person, one of the techniques you can apply is to stand on the shoulder of a giant. In this hobby, there are some giants whom you can stand on their shoulders to see far. You can find then in metal detecting clubs or communities.

After you have found your treasures using your metal detector, the next thing you may think of is how to clean and sell your finds. That will not be any issue because I will educate you in this chapter. I will guide you on how you can sell any treasure you will unearth.

Joining Metal Detecting Club

Many beginners do not understand that one of the major ways they can enhance their detecting skills apart from constant practice is by joining metal detecting clubs. There are many metal detecting clubs that can help you grow. I will list these clubs and you can join any of them to help yourself grow in the field of treasure hunt.

The metal detecting clubs are as follow:

The Warrior Basin Treasure Hunters Association (WBTHA)

This metal detecting club is located in Birmingham, Alabama area, in United States. The purpose of the club is for members to help one another in sharing common interest in metal detecting. The metals they specialize on include detecting of relics, coins, gold, rocks and so on. They have their meeting days. You can join as a member. The club started in the year 1972.

Central Alabama Artifacts Society

This is another metal detecting club you can join without stress. They help one another in skill development. The club is located in Alabama, United States. They usually meet last Tuesday of each month.

Sal's History Hunt Club

Sal's History Hunt or simply put History Hunt Club is a metal detecting hobbyists club. It was founded by Sal Guttuso. Every year, the club members go out for treasures hunting in different countries mainly Americas and Europe. They recommend joining their Facebook group using the name "History Hunts Metal Detecting Group" before signing up for the club. Through their Facebook page, you can meet other experience detectorists.

South East Treasure Hunters

This is another metal detecting club you can join to harness your metal detecting skill. It is located at "789 Brentwood Drive Gadsden, AL, 35901. Members help one another in detecting skill development.

If you are in United Kingdom, there are some UK based metal detecting clubs you can join. Few among them are:

1. Central Searchers Metal Detecting Club
2. Wessex Metal Detecting Association
3. The Magiovinium Metal Detecting Club
4. Cleveland Discoverers and
5. Plymouth Detector Club

How to clean Your Found Coins

I will guide you on how to clean your detected coins which is made either from Silver or Copper. You have to follow this guide to make the coins be as neat as possible.

The steps to follow to clean your coins:

1. Wash your hands properly with soap and water before you start cleaning of your coins
2. Open a tap of water and allow the water to run through the coins to knock away the dirt on the coins surface. Let the water flow at higher intensity.
3. Boil warm water, pour the water in a bowl and then add detergent, and mix properly
4. Add your coins into the mixture and start shaking the bowl containing the coins and the mixture gently. Few coins are to be added.
5. Finally, rinse the coins with distilled water
6. Air-dry the coins or clean the surface gently with soft towel

Other techniques you can use to clean your detected coin are:

1. The use of hot running water
2. Using toothpick or soft bristled toothbrush to remove entrusted dirt from the coins, wash with mixture of hot water and soap, and then air-dry.

Note: Please do not scratch the surface of the coins in the name of cleaning because it will damage them. And when that happens, no buyer will like to buy them.

Step by Step Guide on Cleaning your Detected Jewelry

To clean your jewelry which you detected during treasure hunt, take these few steps:

1. Wash your hands properly with clean soap and water
2. Mix few drops of liquid dish soap with cups of water
3. Place the jewelry in the mixture for some minutes
4. Remove them from the mixture and wash out the mixture with clean distilled water
5. Use soft towel to clean them and allow to air-dry

How to Clean Up Your Gold Find

Gold is a special metal. Because of how precious the metal is, it does not hold much dirt. A Gold is always a Gold.

To clean Gold, just warm water and add small liquid soap. Soak a soft towel in the mixture and use it to clean the Gold. After, allow it to dry in air. Please do not use bleach or ammonia to clean gold because of their harshness.

Cleaning Iron Relics Using Electrolysis Method

Electrolysis has proven to be the best approach to clean Iron relics to good state. The term "electrolysis" is the process of using a direct electrical current to drive an otherwise non-spontaneous chemical reaction". Because Iron relics easily corrode, the need to apply electrolysis as the cleaning approach comes into play.

Electrolytic kit is not that expensive, and you can buy one kit to use for your own cleaning process. You can still make one for yourself if you have the skill. Carry out this metal purification process in a ventilated place. The reason is because Hydrogen gas given out during this process is not good to human health.

The steps to clean your Iron relics using electrolysis process are as follow:

1. Wash the Iron relic and with soap and water, and make sure it is free from oil and sand
2. Pour some water in a plastic bowl and add baking soda inside of it
1. Allow the baking soda to properly dissolve inside the water. The baking soda added is will charge the water. You can stir until it dissolves completely
2. Connect the negative terminal to the Iron relic which you want to clean
3. Connect the positive terminal to the sacrificial metal (the metal to be sacrificed). The metal can be made of Steel. As the electrolysis goes on, the rust on the Iron relics is transferred to sacrificial metal also known as the anode
4. Power on the electrolytic cell using your speed charger
5. Allow the cleaning process to continue
6. Let the process run for at least 8 hours until the rust on the Iron relic is removed. You can set up this process in the night and allow it till daybreak

7. If at a point the anode metal is fully covered up with the rust from the relic, power off the set-up and replace the sacrificial metal with another metal of the same kind (in this example Steel)
8. At the end, power off the electrolytic setup, remove the cleaned Iron relic, wash with clean water and air-dry it

How to preserve Your Iron Relics

You may like to preserve your Iron relics until you contact a buyer. To do so, you can follow this method which I used for my own Iron relics:

1. Dry your relics with oven to the temperature of about 200 degree Celsius
2. Remove the relics using thongs and then pour paraffin oil on it as it is still hot. Do not touch with your hand as you will get hurt because the metal will be hot in that state.
3. Allow the oil to dry inside the relics
4. Use smooth brush to brush the surface

At this state, you have preserved your Iron relics.

How to sell Your Finds

Though many detectorists do not like to sell their finds, some still do. You can sell different kind of finds to different people.

1. You can sell your finds to shops. You can sell your detected coins, Gold, jewelry and Silver to different shops online or offline. Check around your area.
2. You can sell your old coins to coin dealer. The amount they will buy depends on the value placed on the coins.
3. You can sell your old coins to websites that buy them.
4. You can sell your artifacts and old coins to museums that need them
5. Gold and Silver dealers are always ready to buy such precious metals from you.

Appreciation

Thanks for reading.

Index

A

accessories, *67*
All metal, *13*
apply caution, *24*
Assay, *17*

B

Beach Metal Detectors, *63*
Beat-frequency Oscillator, *5*, *6*, *12*
beeps, *2*, *6*, *16*, *53*
BFO, *5*, *6*, *7*, *12*
Black dirt, *14*, *15*
Black sand, *15*
Bounty Hunter, *37*, *38*, *39*, *40*, *41*, *48*, *51*, *53*, *58*, *59*, *63*
Bounty Hunter Metal Detectors, *37*
Bounty Hunter Platinum, *48*, *63*
Bucketlister, *15*

C

Cache, *15*
Canslaw, *16*
Choppy, *14*
Clad, *16*
coin shooting, *50*, *52*
Coin Spill, *17*
Coinball, *16*
Color, *16*

D

Depth Indicator, *31*
Depth Select, 40
detecting hobbyist, *3*, *5*, *45*, *51*, *60*, *67*
Digger, *69*

E

electrolysis, *77*, *78*, *79*
Electrolysis, *77*
Excalibur II metal detector, *54*

F

Find, *14*, *65*, *77*
finding treasures, *5*, *9*
finds, *1*, *3*, *4*, *5*, *9*, *10*, *23*, *27*, *28*, *37*, *38*, *56*, *61*, *70*, *73*, *79*, *80*
fine, *23*
First Texas Products, *41*, *42*
Fisher Lab, *42*

G

Garrett, *43*, *44*, *48*, *49*, *51*, *53*, *58*, *59*, *63*
Garrett metal detectors, *43*
Gold Detecting, *55*, *56*

H

Headphones, *69*

I

Identifying Your Coins, *65*
induction balance, *7*

J

jargon, *12*, *56*

K

Kids, *57*

L

law, *20, 22*
Lingo, *12*
Low tone, *14*

M

Magnetic mineralization intensity, *31*
Makro Multi-Kruzer, *63*
manual, *32, 42, 43, 54, 64*
metal detector, *1, 2, 3, 4, 5, 6, 7, 8, 10, 12, 13, 14, 17, 19, 24, 26, 28, 29, 30, 31, 32, 33, 34, 36, 37, 38, 39, 40, 41, 42, 43, 44, 48, 50, 52, 53, 54, 55, 57, 58, 59, 62, 63, 64, 67, 68, 69, 70, 73*
Metal detector Bags, *67*
Military Zones, *24*
Minelab Excalibur II, *53, 54*
Minelab metal detectors, *35, 36, 37*
multi-frequency metal detectors, *54*

P

Pennyweight, *17*
permission, *22, 25, 26, 72*
PI, *8, 13*
Pinpointer, *17, 67*
Plug, *18*
Pulse Induction, *5, 8, 13, 57*

R

receiver coil, *7*
Relic Hunters, *18*
rules, *22, 23*

S

Safety, *45, 46*
search coil, *3, 4, 6, 19, 29, 30, 32, 33, 35, 38, 43, 53*
Search coil, *29*
Sensitivity, *38*
sensor, *2*

T

TARGET REJECT, *41*
Tone ID, *13*
Tot-lot, *18*
transmitter and **receiver** coils, *7*
Transmitter coil, *7*
Trash management, *20*
trespass, *11, 23*
trespassing, *20, 22*
Troubleshooting, *33*
Types of Metal Detector, *5*

U

underwater, *53, 54, 55*

V

Very Low Frequency, *5, 7, 8, 13, 37, 62*
Visual ID, *13*
VLF, *7, 8, 12, 37, 39, 62*

W

Warranty, *38*

Ingram Content Group UK Ltd.
Milton Keynes UK
UKHW021309300623
424357UK00018B/560